Prayers of Confessions for Lent

Leoma Gilley

Prayers of Confessions for Lent

by
Leoma Gilley

ALL RIGHTS RESERVED. Reproduction of the whole or any part of the contents without written permission is prohibited. Copyright © 2021 by Leoma Gilley. Unless otherwise indicated, all Scripture quotations are taken from the Holy Bible, New Living Translation, copyright © 1996, 2004, 2007, 2013, 2015 by Tyndale House Foundation. Used by permission of Tyndale House Publishers, Inc., Carol Stream, Illinois 60188. All rights reserved.

Cover and book design: Howell Graphics
Editing: Jan Camburn

Any errors in the text are the responsibility of the author.
Library of Congress Control Number: 2021901500

ISBN: 978-1-970037-64-7
ISBN: 978-1-970037-65-4
ISBN: 978-1-970037-66-1

Crippled Beagle Publishing
Knoxville, Tennessee

Printed in the United States of America

Dedication

Susanne Hassell and the Order of St. Brigit

When I was a lonely missionary returning to the US after many years in Africa, I was in desperate need of a community. Susanne warmly received me and provided a way for me to become part of a loving community of women. The Order of St. Brigit includes women who are seeking to become more contemplative by learning to be still, listen to God through the Scriptures, and hold one another accountable to their chosen spiritual disciplines. Susanne is now in heaven after a long struggle with cancer. I'm blessed to still have my sisters in theOrder, part of the New Monasticism. The Order of St. Brigit continues, reaching out to all those who long for more of Christ, for stillness, for peace, for supportive relationships, and for wholeness. Find us here: https://www.facebook.com/orderstbrigit

Introduction

In 2020, I had been pondering what practice I should commit to for Lent. As I attended an Ash Wednesday service at a local Anglican church, I suddenly knew what I needed to do. Each day, I needed to write a prayer of confession.

The purpose of Lent is to spend 40 days from Ash Wednesday until Easter (not including Sundays) preparing ourselves for the celebration of Easter. In order to more fully capture the significance of Jesus' death on the cross for us, we should be aware of the sins, both intentional and unintentional, that we have committed and for which we need forgiveness. By the time we arrive at Good Friday, we should be ever so much more grateful for the price that was paid for our sins.

The prayers in this small book are certainly not a complete compilation of areas in which we need forgiveness, but there should be some familiar topics as well as some we may not have considered. Each of the prayers is based on Scripture, inspired by the New Living Translation. Other Lenten practices may include fasting (abstaining from food and/or some activities), sacrificing purchases of personal wants and donating that money to good causes, spending more time in God's Word, or reflecting on his promises, volunteering, or committing to any other practice that would demonstrate the mercy and love of God to those around us. It should be noted that Sundays are not included in the 40 days of Lent because Sunday is always a celebration of resurrection. On those days, there are prayers of praise and thanks.

For other explanations about Lent, you may want to look at this resource: https://www.cru.org/us/en/train-and-grow/life-and-relationships/ holidays/lent/what-is-lent-about-and-why-is-it-important.html https://www.crosswalk.com/faith/spiritual-life/lent-101-honoring- the-sacrifice-of-jesus-1382259.html
https://christianity.org.uk/article/what-is-lent
https://www.umc.org/en/content/ask-the-umc-what-is-lent-and-why-does-it-last-forty-days

Ash Wednesday: General confession

"Have mercy on us, O God, because of your unfailing love.
Because of your great compassion, blot out the stain of our sins.
Wash us clean from our guilt.
Purify us from our sin, for we recognize our rebellion.
It haunts us day and night.
Against you, and you alone, have we sinned;
we have done what is evil in your sight.
You will be proved right in what you say,
and your judgment against us is just."

LORD, in your mercy, hear our prayer.
Based on Psalm 51:1-4

Community

LORD, you have placed us in communities.
Sometimes we get along with our neighbors,
and sometimes we don't.
However, you will judge us on how we reach out to others,
whether we feed the hungry,
help the sick,
offer hospitality to the stranger,
or turn away.
When we have done these things
for our neighbors,
you consider that we did them to you.
Forgive us
for the times we have opted to keep to ourselves
and not reached out to those around us.
Help us to be more intentional and open to being
a blessing to those in our communities.

LORD, in your mercy, hear our prayer.
Based on Matthew 25:35-40

Keeping the Sabbath

LORD, we confess
that we have not kept the Sabbath holy
as you instructed us to do.
We have pursued our own interests and business,
despite your giving us a day
to rest and enjoy times of worship
and communion with family and friends.
Forgive us for not honoring
you each week as we should.
Thank you for the promise
that if we follow your command in this regard,
we will find you to be our delight.

LORD, in your mercy, hear our prayer.
Based on Isaiah 58:13-14

Selfishness

O LORD, we see the earth mourn and dry up as crops wither.
None of us will escape your judgment.
Why is this happening?
You have told us that the earth suffers
because of the sins of its people.
We have twisted your instructions,
violated your laws,
and broken your everlasting covenant.
As a result, a curse consumes the earth,
and we must pay the price for our sin.
Forgive us for our lack of care
for the world you have given us.
Because of our greed and selfishness,
we have caused other inhabitants of this earth to suffer.
O LORD, we need your forgiveness!

LORD, in your mercy, hear our prayer.
Based on Isaiah 24:2-6

Sunday #1

Thank you, LORD,
for loving us so much
that you sent your one and only Son
to offer us the opportunity
for eternal life
through faith in Jesus.
Thank you
that the Son
didn't come to judge the world
but to save the world.
Thank you for saving us.

Based on John 3:16-17

Faith

When the disciples came back to Jesus
with only five loaves of bread and two fish,
I'm sure they felt this amount of food
was totally inadequate for them,
let alone the 5,000 other people
who were hungry.
We expect that the boy
who gave the bread and fish
also felt it was too small an offering
to do any good.
Forgive us for our lack of faith
in what you can do with the little
that we have to offer.
Increase our faith and our willingness
to give back to you
what you have first given to us.

LORD, in your mercy, hear our prayer.
Based on Luke 9:13-17

Time for Listening to God

LORD, all too often our busy lives crowd you out. We may be unwilling to get up early enough to make time for you before our activities begin, and we fail to stop until the end of the day.
By that time, we're tired
and don't wish to concentrate.
Forgive us for not making time with you a priority.
You spent nights in prayer, and we fail to spend half an hour with you.
Help us to pray with all our hearts
and to obey your laws.
Move us to rise early to cry out for help
and put our hope in your words.
When we wake up in the night, may our minds
be focused on your promises.
Let us be revived as we draw closer to you.

LORD, in your mercy, hear our prayer.
Based on Psalm 119:145-149

Bigotry

Forgive us
for our anger, bitterness, hatred,
prejudice, and bigotry toward others
who are different from us.
Jesus, you have commanded us to love our enemies
and do good to those who hate us.
We are to bless those who curse us
and pray for those who hurt us.
You've told us to treat others
as we would like them to treat us.
Forgive us, LORD, when
we reject others because they are somehow
different from us, either by the color of their skin,
their sexual orientation, or their beliefs.
Help us not to live in fear and prejudice,
but to reach out to others and be open, caring people
who demonstrate your love for ALL people.

LORD, in your mercy, hear our prayer.
Based on Luke 6:27-30

Complacency

LORD, we confess
that we have been complacent in our Christianity.
Therefore, we pray for ourselves
and those in your church
who have not been hot or cold but lukewarm
toward fulfilling your command
to go into all the world and preach the gospel.
We have thought of ourselves as rich,
not in need of anything because we have the means
to buy and enjoy everything we want.
We have failed to see ourselves as you see us:
wretched, miserable, poor, and blind.
Help us to be changed in our thoughts and actions,
to see ourselves as you see us,
and to receive your discipline.
Cause us to be diligent in following you.
Cause us to actively spread your Good News
to all the world. Forgive us for our indifference.

LORD, in your mercy, hear our prayer.
Based on Revelation 1:15-19

Holding to our Convictions

Thank you, LORD,
for the model of Daniel and his friends
who determined not to sin against you
and the commands you had given to the Israelites
about what they should eat.
We are constantly tempted to eat things
that are not healthy for us,
to engage in practices that are not good for us,
and all too often we give in to those temptations.
We forget that our bodies are your temples.
We need to remember that you live in us
and walk among us.
Be our God and make us people who honor and glorify you.

LORD, in your mercy, hear our prayer.
Based on Daniel 1:8 and 2 Corinthians 6:16

Responding to God's Call

LORD, you call us
to come and listen to your counsel.
You desire to share
your heart with us and make us wise.
You often call us,
but we do not come.
You reach out to us,
but we pay no attention
and ignore your advice,
  rejecting the correction you offer.
Forgive us, LORD,
that we seem to hate knowledge
and we choose not to fear you, the LORD.

LORD, in your mercy, hear our prayer.
Based on Proverbs 1:23-25, 29

Sunday #2

We praise you, God,
because you are light
and there is no darkness in you at all.
Thank you for the promise
that if we live in the light
as you are in the light,
we have fellowship with each other,
and the blood of Jesus, your Son,
cleanses us from all sin.

Based on 1 John 1:5, 7

Unfaithfulness and Disobedience

LORD, forgive us
for our pride,
vanity,
and hypocrisy.
You have cautioned us
that pride goes before
destruction and
haughtiness before a fall.
You do not allow
haughtiness in heaven,
but you welcome those who are humble
and never tell lies
or deceive one another.
Help us to be the humble people you want us to be.

LORD, in your mercy, hear our prayer.
Based on Proverbs 16:18 and Zephaniah 3:11-13

Self-pity, Impatience, and Envy

Father, forgive
us when our motivations for success
are because we envy what our neighbors have.
This is foolishness
because we are created
to follow the path you have for us.
Jealousy and selfishness
are not your kind of wisdom.
Our desires are earthly, unspiritual, and unworthy.
Wherever there is jealousy or selfish ambition,
there we will find disorder and evil of every kind.
Instead, help us to seek wisdom from above
that directs us to being peace-loving, gentle,
willing to yield to others, and
full of mercy and good deeds.
Help us to plant seeds of peace
so that we may reap a harvest of righteousness.

LORD, in your mercy, hear our prayer.
Based on Ecclesiastes 4:4 and James 3:15-18

Abortions

LORD, you made
all the delicate, inner parts
of our bodies and put us together in our mothers' wombs.
You watched us as we were being formed in utter seclusion
and wove us together in the dark.
Every day of our lives was recorded in your book,
every moment laid out before
a single day had passed.
But we have cut many of those lives short
because children didn't figure into our plans.
We have legalized death
rather than accept responsibility for our actions.
We have not seen children as a gift
but as a burden. Change our perspectives
and our values so that we may no longer
dishonor you by these actions.

LORD, in your mercy, hear our prayer.
Based on Psalm 139:13-16

Pride

LORD,
all too often we have loved this world
and the things it offers
more than we have loved you.
We confess
that we have craved physical pleasure
and lusted for the things we see.
We have allowed ourselves to be proud
of our achievements and possessions,
even though all of these come from you.
Remind us that this world is fading away,
along with everything people crave.
Help us to remember that all things come from you.
May our response be humility, deep gratitude, and
a longing for our true eternal home.

LORD, in your mercy, hear our prayer.
Based on 1 John 1:15-17

Civil Discourse

LORD, we cry out to you
because of the divisions among people in this nation.
Many people earn their living
fomenting discord and hatred of others.
Violence is everywhere,
and we need your salvation.
There is so much misery we can barely stand to look.
Destruction and violence are everywhere.
We are surrounded by people who love to argue and fight.
The law has become paralyzed.
There is no justice in the courts.
It seems the wicked outnumber the righteous so much so
that justice has become perverted.
LORD, have mercy and bring us to repentance
for our parts in this failure to be civil and respectful.
Help us to seek the truth,
be willing to listen to each other,
and speak the truth in love.

LORD, in your mercy, hear our prayer.
Based on Habakkuk 1:2-4

Living as Holy People

God, you have told us
to be the holy people you love,
and as such we should be
merciful, kind, humble, gentle, and patient.
We should make allowances for others' faults
and forgive anyone who offends us.
All too often we are not like this.
You have forgiven us so much,
but we have failed to forgive others in the same way;
so, we humbly ask for your forgiveness.
Help us to clothe ourselves with your love
which will bind us all together in perfect harmony.
May we let your peace rule in our hearts.
Help us to be good representatives of the Lord Jesus.

LORD, in your mercy, hear our prayer.
Based on Colossians 3:12-17

Sunday #3

Thank you, LORD,
for giving us glimpses
of what heaven will be like.
We read that,
"No eye has seen,
no ear has heard,
and no mind has imagined
what God has prepared
for those who love him."
May we focus more often
on the blessings
you have promised us
and rejoice
in the eternal life you offer.

Based on 1 Corinthians 2:9-12

Repentance and Returning

LORD, we weep for those times when we have failed to follow you
and instead have yielded to the temptation
to follow the enemy of our souls.
We pray that we will frequently
come back to you and find hope.
In some cases, you may have to severely discipline us
to cause us to turn again to you so that we may be restored.
You alone are the LORD our God,
and we have turned away from you.
Make us truly sorry.
May we kick ourselves for our stupidity!
We confess we are thoroughly ashamed
of what we did in our younger days.
Thank you that even though you punish us you still love us
and long for us. Thank you for your mercy.
May we acknowledge that you are the One True God
and that as we return to you, you have promised to give
rest to the weary and joy to the sorrowful.

LORD, in your mercy, hear our prayer.
Based on Jeremiah 31:16-25

Obedience

LORD,
we are experiencing a world-wide crisis with lots of uncertainty,
yet you call us to minister to those with whom we interact
in the course of our lives.
When we hear your call in such situations, it is tempting to respond as
Moses did, "LORD, please, send anyone else."
Forgive us for our reticence,
hesitation, and resistance to obey your call
to serve you by serving others.

LORD, in your mercy, hear our prayer.
Based on Exodus 4:13

Misplaced Trust

LORD,
our eyes are so often focused
on what is around us rather than on you.
We trust in what our own hands
have made and in all we have accumulated—
our bank accounts, stocks, and bonds.
We rely too much on our abilities,
power, or strength.
This attitude is just like worshiping
at a pagan shrine.
We have forgotten the Rock
who can hide us in times of trouble.
We have turned away
from the God who can save us.
Forgive us, O LORD,
and cause us to turn our eyes to you,
our Creator, the Holy One.

LORD, in your mercy, hear our prayer.
Based on Isaiah 17:7-10

Treatment of the Poor

LORD,
we know the poor and oppressed
cry out to you,
and you have commanded us
to respond to their needs.
Forgive us for failing
to defend the oppressed or
failing to show pity
for the weak and the needy.
Cause us to rescue them and
help redeem them from violence,
for their lives are precious to you.
Remind us that if we shut our ears
to the cries of the poor,
you may ignore us in our own times of need.

LORD, in your mercy, hear our prayer.
Based on Psalm 72:12-14, Proverbs 21:13

National Repentance

LORD,
you have called us to ask
for the old, godly way and walk in it.
If we travel its path we will find rest for our souls,
but we have replied,
"No, that's not the road we want!"
You sent godly people to warn us to listen to the sound of the alarm.
But we replied, "No! We won't pay attention!"
As a result of our hard hearts, you have decided
to bring disaster on us. This disaster will be the fruit of our own
schemes because we refuse to listen to you, God.
We have rejected your Word. So, you tell us you will
put obstacles in our paths. Parents and children
will both fall over them. Neighbors and friends will die together.
LORD, forgive us and our nation for our sins,
and turn us back to be obedient to your Word.

LORD, in your mercy, hear our prayer.
Based on Jeremiah 6:16-21

True Fasting

LORD, we confess
that fasting (doing without food for a time) is not popular these days,
but you have also said that what is more important
is to stop oppressing employees
and to stop quarreling.
We may bow our heads
and go through the motions of penance,
but if our hearts are not in it,
there is nothing to be gained by it.
Help us to free those wrongly imprisoned,
lighten the burden of those who work for us,
let the oppressed go free, and remove the chains that bind people.
Remind us to share our food with the hungry,
give shelter to the homeless,
and offer clothes to those who need them.
May we be open and available to others,
especially to family members who need our help.
Then you will be able to truly bless us.

LORD, in your mercy, hear our prayer.
Based on Isaiah 58:4-7

Sunday #4

Thank you, LORD,
that when righteous people earnestly pray to you
those prayers have great power
and produce wonderful results.
Thank you
that we have the privilege
to come to you in prayer
through our LORD Jesus Christ.

Based on James 5:16

Calling on God for Help

LORD,
we find ourselves in the midst of storms in our lives,
and we try to handle things by ourselves.
We eventually realize we are going to go under,
and we finally cry out to you.
We think you don't care that we are struggling,
when really you are just waiting
for us to ask for help.
Once asked, you can still the storm
and produce calm.
It may not be the solution we were thinking of,
but your answer is the one we need.
Forgive us for being afraid and showing a lack of faith in you.
Help us to realize your great power and authority.

LORD, in your mercy, hear our prayer.
Based on Mark 4:38-41

Rejecting Truth

LORD, we confess to you
that the day has now arrived
in our nation and in our world
when people no longer want to listen to sound
and wholesome teaching.
We want to follow our own desires
and look for teachers
who will tell us whatever we want to hear.
We reject the truth
and chase after myths.
Open our ears, eyes,
and hearts
to listen for your truth
and to turn from our self-deceiving ways.

LORD, in your mercy, hear our prayer.
Based on 2 Timothy 4:3-4

Oppression

LORD,
the desire for money and power
has led many to abuse the people who work for them
or even people who live with them.
They choose the good things for themselves,
even taking away what rightfully belongs to others,
leaving the remnants for those doing the real work.
These workers are abused and misused,
and too often we are responsible
for allowing that to continue.
LORD, forgive us and help us
change our priorities, attitudes, and actions
to be in line with your values.
When we see wrongdoing happening,
give us the courage to speak up for those
whose voices have been silenced by oppression.

LORD, in your mercy, hear our prayer.
Based on Ezekiel 34:18-22

Forgiveness

LORD God, our Father,
you have forgiven us for so much
that we can never begin to repay you.
We have failed
to forgive others who offend us
or we have failed
to make allowance for their faults.
Forgive
the tendency to hold grudges
and our failure to truly love
those who have offended or angered us.
Help us to clothe ourselves with love
so that we may live in
peace and harmony with others.

LORD, in your mercy, hear our prayer.
Based on Colossians 3:13-14

Self-indulgence

LORD,
we are guilty of indulging ourselves at every turn.
We get involved in foolish discussions
and end up arguing and saying things we later regret.
We store up goods in large amounts,
thus depriving others.
We pursue worldly goods
because we don't want to be uncomfortable.
Forgive us for our selfish thoughts and actions.
Help us to be honest and serious in our prayers
so that we may grow and mature
in righteousness, faith,
love, and peace.
Help us to listen to others
with gentleness and to
stay calm in the midst of disagreement.
May we run from Satan's trap when temptations come.

LORD, in your mercy, hear our prayer.
Based on 2 Timothy 2:22-26

Blindness to Human Need and Suffering

LORD, forgive us for our indifference to injustice and cruelty
and for our blindness to human need and suffering.
When we have seen invaders come and carry off people's wealth,
we have stood aloof and refused to help them.
When our fellow humans have sought refuge
in a distant land, we have delighted in our superiority,
our own citizenship, and our rights.
When others have suffered misfortune,
we have rejoiced in our fortunes.
When others have suffered calamity, we have gloated
over their destruction or taken advantage of them.
When survivors have sought to escape death,
we have stood in their way and prevented
their finding a place of safety.
We have even returned them to the place and circumstances that
caused their suffering.
Open our eyes, LORD.
Grant us repentance and give us compassion.

LORD, in your mercy, hear our prayer.
Based on Obadiah 1:10-14

Sunday # 5

LORD, we praise you and honor you,
for you have not ignored or belittled
the suffering of the needy.
You have not turned away from them
but have heard their cries for help.
We praise you
that you have rescued us
and helped us in times of
uncertainty and danger.
We also praise you for your sacrifice
that Jesus made for our very souls.
We bow before you.
All power and glory belong to you.

Based on Psalm 22:23-25

Jealousy

How often do we follow
the pattern of the apostle Peter
when he asked Jesus,
"Lord, what about him?"
We are too concerned
about what others may have
and we lack,
or that they may get some reward
we think we deserve.
We wonder what others think of us
rather than express concern
with what you think of us.
Forgive us for our self-centeredness.
Turn our thoughts away from ourselves
and more toward you.

LORD, in your mercy, hear our prayer.
Based on John 21:21

Love of Money and Possessions

LORD, we confess
that we have grown tired of serving you
and have turned our worship
to the things of this world.
In fact,
we have so come to love our possessions and riches
that we cheat to get more.
We use trickery, extortion, and even violence,
and we no longer tell the truth.
We deserve your wrath and judgment.
Before you destroy us,
turn our hearts back to you that we may do what is right,
love mercy, and walk humbly in your presence.

LORD, in your mercy, hear our prayer.
Based on Micah 6:8-12

Gossip

LORD, forgive us
for our tendency to gossip,
sometimes in the form of requesting prayer.
We have harmed our neighbors
and spoken evil of our friends.
We have broken our promises
because we haven't truly cared more
for our friends, family, or colleagues
than we have for ourselves.
Help us to lead blameless lives
and do what is right,
always speaking the truth from sincere hearts.

LORD, in your mercy, hear our prayer.
Based on Psalm 15

Pride

If we claim we have not sinned,
we are just fooling ourselves
and not living in the truth.
So, LORD,
help us to own up to our sins,
confess them to you,
and be forgiven.
Cleanse us from all wickedness.
Don't let us call you a liar
by claiming we have not sinned,
for that would mean
that your Word has no place in us.

LORD, in your mercy, hear our prayer.
Based on 1 John 1:8-10

Willfulness

LORD,
all of us, like sheep,
have strayed away.
We have left your plan
so we can follow our own desires.
We have been rebellious,
deceitful, and proud.
These choices have left us
broken people in desperate need
of healing and wholeness.
Our minds are confused,
and what we see as straight
is often very crooked.
We acknowledge that
Jesus' death on the cross covers these sins
and can make us whole.
Thank you for your sacrifice.
Heal us, O LORD, for we are truly in need.

LORD, in your mercy, hear our prayer.
Based on Isaiah 53:4-8

Counting the Cost

O LORD,
some of us have not really counted
the cost of following you.
We have said we are your followers,
but we have not actually followed very well.
When trials and suffering come along,
we are disappointed in you
because our lives are not easy and straightforward.
You have not promised us "easy."
You warned us that the way
would be hard and
we would suffer as Jesus did.
Still, you order us to
take up our crosses daily and follow you.
Forgive us for our half-hearted devotion
and our unwillingness to give up
the comforts we enjoy in order
to completely devote ourselves to you.

LORD, in your mercy, hear our prayer.
Based on Luke 14:26-27

Sunday #6

Thank you, LORD,
that we have reached this point in time.
We are still working
to finish our races
and remain faithful.
We look forward to
the prizethat
awaits us—
the crown of righteousness,
which you, Jesus,
have made possible for us.
We look forward to your return
and rejoice that you are coming for us.

Based on 2 Timothy 4:8

Expectations

LORD, we confess
that our expectations are not realistic.
We expect that WE will never die,
that suffering will not be part of OUR world,
and that being jobless will not be part of OUR present or future.
We expect to be able to meet with friends and family,
for doctors to be able to fix our health problems,
and for life to continue as normal. Children will be in school.
We can choose whether or not to attend church.
We expect our meetings will continue unhindered.
We confess that you have shown us in these days
how quickly our lives and expectations can change
and how important certain people,
who have had little recognition in the past, really are.
Forgive us for our selfishness and lack of appreciation
for the world we had and the people who made it possible. You have
reminded us of our need for you. Help us to take you seriously and
turn back to you, our Creator.

LORD, in your mercy, hear our prayer.
Based on Isaiah 17:4-8

Love our Neighbors

LORD,
the second greatest commandment
is to love our neighbor as we love ourselves.
We confess that we have not done that.
We have loved ourselves well,
but we have often failed
to reach out to our neighbors,
to forgive them when they annoy or aggravate us,
and to teach them your Good News.
Help us to follow your example
by loving even those who hate us.

LORD, in your mercy, hear our prayer.
Based on Mark 12:31

A Holy Life

LORD,
you have told us
that we are to live as your obedient children,
yet we must confess that we slip back
into our old ways of living
and satisfying our own desires.
Before we belonged to you,
we didn't know any better.
Now we do know better,
and we are called to be holy
in all that we do—being holy just as you are holy.
Remind us that we are only temporary residents here.
You paid a HUGE ransom to save us
from our empty, meaningless lives.
That ransom was paid
by the precious blood of Christ.
Forgive our laxity and indifference.
Guide us into your holiness.

LORD, in your mercy, hear our prayer.
Based on 1 Peter 1:14-19

Mind Control

LORD, we confess
that we have allowed our sinful nature
to control our minds,
which we know leads to death.
We have been hostile to you and your laws.
Thus, we cannot please you.
Fortunately, you have given us the path
to life and peace
if we allow the Spirit to lead us.
Help us to allow you
to exercise control over our minds and bodies
so that, through the power of the Spirit,
you will put to death the deeds of our sinful nature.
And thus, we will truly live and
be grateful children of God.

LORD, in your mercy, hear our prayer.
Based on Romans 8:6-14

Living out our Intentions

LORD,
you call us so often
to come and talk with you.
You offer us refuge
when troubles come.
You will hide us in your sanctuary
and place us on a high rock
out of the reach of our troubles.
And in response,
we say, "LORD, I'm coming."
But we don't come.
We mean to,
but we get distracted or busy or lazy.
LORD, please don't reject us in anger
or turn your back on us. Don't abandon us.
Hold us close. Teach us how to live out our intentions.
Help us follow the right path so that we see your goodness
while we are here in the land of the living.

LORD, in your mercy, hear our prayer.
Based on Psalm 27

Self-importance

LORD, we confess
that we often think the world revolves around us,
and that it can't go on without us.
In truth, everything we have comes from you.
We have only what you first gave us!
We are only on this earth for a moment,
like visitors and strangers in this land.
Our days are like a passing shadow,
gone so soon without a trace.
So, LORD, help us to always want to obey you.
See to it that our love for you never changes
and that we are constantly aware of
your mercy and grace for us.

LORD, in your mercy, hear our prayer.
Based on 1 Chronicles 29:14-15, 18

Easter

Yours, O LORD,
is the greatness,
the power,
the glory,
the victory,
and the majesty.
Everything in the heavens and on earth
is yours, O LORD,
and this is your kingdom.
We adore you as the one
who is over all things.
Wealth and honor come from you alone,
for you rule over everything.
Power and might are in your hand,
and at your discretion people are made great
and given strength. O our God, we thank you
and praise your glorious name!

LORD, in your mercy, hear our prayer.
Based on 1 Chronicles 29:11-1

Other Books by Leoma Gilley

The Still Small Voice of Love:
A journey into a deeper relationship with Jesus
In this thought and prayer-provoking devotional, author Leoma Gilley leads readers through the Lectio Divina method to study Scripture andlisten for God's responses.

An Autosegmental Approach to Shilluk Phonology
(SIL Internationaland the University of Texas at Arlington Publications in Linguistics, Vol 103)

Praying for Big Things
Having been challenged by a colleague to pray for situations in the world that are really serious, she sought to develop prayers based onscripture to pray God's words back to him. This book doesn't cover everything, but it is a beginning, and Leoma hopes it will help to enrichand deepen your prayer life as it has hers.

Every Day But Not Some, Glimpses Into the
Everyday Lives of Sudanese

Reports about the Sudan are often critical and harsh, and it is easy to equate the people of the Sudan with their government's policies. By contrast, the stories in Every Day But Not Some offer a more positive view of what life is like for the ordinary Sudanese.

Notes

www.ingramcontent.com/pod-product-compliance
Lightning Source LLC
Chambersburg PA
CBHW071423070526
44578CB00003B/677